# LITTLE CAFÉ CAKES

Penguin Books (NZ) Ltd, cnr Airborne and Rosedale
Roads, Albany, Auckland 1310, New Zealand
Penguin Books Ltd, 27 Wrights Lane,
London W8 5TZ, England
Penguin Putnam Inc, 375 Hudson Street, New York,
NY 10014, United States
Penguin Books Australia Ltd, 487 Maroondah Highway,
Ringwood, Australia 3134
Penguin Books Canada Ltd, 10 Alcorn Avenue, Toronto,
Ontario, Canada M4V3B2
Penguin Books (South Africa) Pty Ltd, 5 Watkins Street,
Denver Ext 4, 2094, South Africa
Penguin Books India (P) Ltd, 11, Community Centre,
Panchsheel Park, New Delhi 110 017, India
Penguin Books Ltd, Registered Offices: Harmondsworth,
Middlesex, England

First published by Penguin Books (NZ) Ltd, 2001
10 9 8 7 6 5 4 3

Copyright © text, Julie Le Clerc, 2001
Copyright © photographs, Penguin Books (NZ) Ltd, 2001
The right of Julie Le Clerc to be identified as the author
of this work in terms of section 96 of the Copyright Act
1994 is hereby asserted.

Designed and typeset by Athena Sommerfeld
Printed by Condor Production, Hong Kong

ISBN 0 14100414 2

# LITTLE CAFÉ CAKES

Julie Le Clerc
**Photography Shaun Cato-Symonds**

PENGUIN BOOKS

My thanks go to so many unsung heroes for their support; you know who you are and how much you mean to me. Special thanks again go to Shaun Cato-Symonds for your beautiful and perceptive photography in this book as with the previous ones. Thank you Katrina Tanner for your hands, poise, patience and insightful gems of wisdom, and young Katie Edwards, my little Alice in Wonderland holding the sweet wee cakes that say EAT ME. Thank you Rachel Carley for supplying me with even more pretty china. My thanks and applause go to Athena Sommerfeld for your delicate design skills and this book's exquisite arrangement. And thank you Bernice Beachman and Philippa Gerrard, the talented team at Penguin Books (NZ) for such thoughtful editorial assistance.

## contents

6   INTRODUCTION

8   IMPORTANT NOTES

10  STRAIGHT CHOCOLATE

23  SYRUP DRENCHED

36  FRUIT AND VEG

49  NUTTY VARIETIES

62  GRAINS AND RICE

75  BREAD AND BUTTER

88  CHEESECAKES

102 INDEX

## introduction

I have a small collection of old cake tins, the kind that could always be relied upon, the kind that were always full. I cherish them for the misty memories they now hold and for the style of food they once held. Sturdy tin containers with quaint and now faded images and pure home baking remind me nostalgically of my grandmother, a certain softness that was part of her, her warm heart and the fragrance of her cooking. She would always have small special treats of my most favourite flavours waiting for when I visited.

I have observed that singular items of food tend to be most popular. I'm not quite sure why but I think this yearning may be attributed to any number of similarly evocative or sentimental reasons peculiar to individuals. There is something very special about having a tenderly formed small creation all to oneself. Little cakes needn't be fancy, precious nor sickly sweet for heaven's sake. A little treat, however, can provide the sweetest pleasure.

Good home-baked products are the most delicious, but finding trusted recipes or stimulating ideas is not easy. I know many home cooks and professional bakers who are constantly searching for quality, inexpensive and reliable recipes. This book provides ideas for straightforward recipes that result in an array of smart little cakes with seriously good flavours. Following the popularity of (dare I mention the word) muffins, small individual cakes are even more appealing for many reasons. They are just as quick and easy to prepare but produce a superior result. Little cakes have a more pleasing texture and complexity of flavour; they are more attractive and can be enhanced further by decorating with simple icings, syrups, fruit or sauces.

Little cakes charm all age groups and are incredibly inviting. They are the perfect in-between treat, or lunch-box, mid-morning or afternoon-tea snack. Their versatility means these sweet little things can double as wonderful desserts. Baby cakes are so totally irresistible some people have been known to eat them for breakfast! And why not, I say. Herein lies an opportunity to indulge in a little fancy of your choosing and refill those memory-laden cake tins while providing pleasure to all who enjoy a little sweetness in life.

important notes

- Individual cake tins used are of a $^3/_4$ (180ml) cup capacity filled to $^3/_4$.

- Be sure to grease tins well and line with non-stick baking paper if advised to do so. Do not over-fill the tins or they will spill their contents into the oven. This is not a pretty sight.

- All recipes yield baby cakes but substitute tin sizes are given for cooking as large cakes where appropriate. Timing is only given for little cakes, as this is a book about little cakes. Baking times may vary for larger cakes. As a guide allow 45—60 minutes and start testing at intervals from 45 minutes until a skewer inserted comes out clean.

- All cakes were tested in a fan-forced oven. Increase temperature by 10°C if using a conventional oven.

- All measurements for spoons or cups are for level, loosely packed amounts unless otherwise stated.

- All eggs are small (New Zealand size 6) unless otherwise stated.

- As these cakes are small they can easily become dry if overcooked. It is advisable to test cakes carefully towards the end of cooking time as even a few minutes for a small cake can cause near ruin. I can offer one small hint as a way of reviving any cake that may be a little dry. That is, to drench it in a hot syrup and hope for the best. Choose an appropriately flavoured syrup to complement the cake (see chapter two).

- Many toppings, syrups, frostings and icings are interchangeable.

straight chocolate

## sour cream cocoa cakes

A hint of sourness actually complements chocolate beautifully.

100g butter

1 cup sugar

1 tsp vanilla extract

pinch salt

1 cup sour cream

1 egg, lightly beaten

1 1/4 cups flour

1/4 cup cocoa powder

1 tsp baking soda

1 tsp baking powder

1 Preheat oven to 160°C. Grease and flour 12 individual cake or muffin tins or one 20cm spring-form cake tin.

2 Melt the butter and gently stir in sugar, vanilla, salt, sour cream and egg until blended.

3 Stir in the combined sifted dry ingredients.

4 Divide mixture between prepared tins and bake for 20 minutes or until cakes spring back when gently pressed.

5 Ice with chocolate frosting, see page 18.

**Makes 12**

## additions to this recipe

- Spoon 1/2 tblsp raspberry jam on top of each cake before cooking.
- Hide an extra teaspoonful of sour cream in the centre of each cake before cooking.

## chocolate lamington baby cakes

Experiment with different shaped lamingtons just for fun.

**4 eggs**
**1 cup caster sugar**
**125g plain flour, sifted**
**1 tblsp cocoa powder, sifted**
**1 tblsp butter, melted**

1. Preheat oven to 180°C. Grease and flour 12 individual cake or muffin tins or one 20cm spring-form cake tin.
2. Put eggs and sugar into a bowl and whisk for about 5 minutes until mixture is light and fluffy.
3. Very gently fold sifted flour and cocoa through the mixture, quickly followed by the butter.
4. Pour into prepared tins and bake for 10 minutes until little cakes spring back when pressed.

**Makes 12**

## chocolate coconut coating

**150g quality dark chocolate**
**100g Kremelta/copha (hardened coconut oil)**
**100g desiccated coconut threads**

1. Melt the chocolate and hardened coconut oil together in a double boiler, or microwave for 2 minutes. Stir until smooth.
2. Use a fork or skewer to dip each sponge into liquid chocolate and then roll in coconut. Leave to set on a wire rack.

## little chocolate bleeding hearts

Break the hearts of these sweet things and hot liquid chocolate escapes.

**250g butter**
**250g quality dark chocolate, broken into pieces**
**³/₄ cup sugar**
**1 tsp vanilla extract**
**7 eggs**
**pinch salt**
**7 tblsp plain flour, sifted**

1  Preheat oven to 160°C. Grease and flour 12 individual cake or muffin tins.
2  Gently heat butter and chocolate together in a double boiler or microwave until just melted. Remove from the heat and stir until smooth.
3  Mix in sugar, vanilla, eggs and salt until smooth. Quickly and briefly mix in flour until just blended.
4  Divide batter into prepared tins filling to 3/4 full. Bake for 10 – 15 minutes until edges are set but centres are still very wet and a little sunken.
5  Cool in tins for 5 minutes before carefully removing by running a knife around edge of each cake. Serve immediately so that their hearts bleed when cut.

**Makes 12**

### serving suggestions

● Dust with a mixture of quality cocoa powder and icing sugar.
● Perfect served with clotted or whipped cream.

## little chocolate brownie cakes

A novel way to prepare chocolate brownie while still retaining the classic brownie texture.

**100g butter**
**200g quality dark chocolate, roughly chopped**
**2 eggs, lightly beaten**
**³/₄ cup caster sugar**
**1 cup flour, sifted**
**¹/₂ cup white chocolate bits**

1 Preheat oven to 180°C. Grease and flour 12 individual cake or muffin tins or a small slice tin.
2 Melt butter and chocolate together in a double boiler, or microwave for 2 minutes. Cool a little then stir in the beaten eggs and sugar.
3 Stir in the flour and beat to combine. Stir in the white chocolate bits.
4 Spoon mixture into prepared tins and bake for 25 minutes or until a skewer inserted comes out clean.
5 Dust with icing sugar to serve.

**Makes 12**

### nice things to add to little brownies

- Substitute dark chocolate bits for the white chocolate bits.
- 1/2 cup chopped nuts — try peanuts, walnuts, pistachio nuts, even cashew nuts or almonds.
- 1/2 cup raisins or chopped dried apricots.

## spiced chocolate buttermilk cakes

Buttermilk is widely obtainable in supermarkets and lends these cakes a subtle texture. If cultured buttermilk is not available substitute soured milk, which is made by adding a little vinegar to ordinary milk.

1 cup buttermilk

$1^1/_4$ cups sugar

125g butter, melted

$^1/_4$ cup cocoa powder

$^1/_2$ tsp baking soda

$1^1/_2$ cups self-raising flour

1 tblsp cinnamon

2 eggs, lightly beaten

1 Preheat oven to 160°C. Grease and flour 20 individual cake or muffin tins or one 22cm spring-form cake tin.

2 Combine buttermilk, sugar, butter, cocoa and baking soda in a large pan. Stir over low heat until sugar dissolves.

3 Add sifted flour, cinnamon and eggs and beat well to incorporate. Pour into prepared tins and bake for 25 minutes or until a skewer inserted comes out clean.

4 Remove from tins to cool then ice with chocolate ganache.

**Makes 20**

## chocolate ganache

Ganache holds sublime mouth-appeal both in taste and texture.

$^1/_2$ cup dark chocolate melts

$^1/_2$ cup cream

1 Gently melt chocolate and cream together in microwave or double boiler. Stir to form a smooth sauce. Allow to cool and thicken then spoon over each little cake.

**Makes 1 cup**

## mini chocolate fudge cakes

Gooey, fudgey and completely delicious.

| | |
|---|---|
| 1 cup water | $1^{1}/_{2}$ cups self-raising flour |
| 250g butter | $^{1}/_{4}$ cup cocoa powder |
| 250g dark chocolate | 2 eggs, lightly beaten |
| 2 cups caster sugar | 1 tsp vanilla extract |

1 Preheat oven to 160°C. Grease, flour and line with non-stick baking paper the base of 12 individual cake or muffin tins or one 20cm spring-form cake tin.
2 Combine water, butter, chocolate and sugar together in a saucepan. Stir over a low heat until sugar has dissolved. Cool to room temperature.
3 Sift together flour and cocoa, and gently stir into chocolate mixture. Lightly whisk in beaten eggs and vanilla.
4 Pour into prepared cake tins. Bake for 20 – 25 minutes or until a skewer inserted comes out clean. Cool before removing from tins.
5 Ice with chocolate frosting.

**Makes 12**

## chocolate frosting

**150g butter**
**1 cup chopped dark chocolate or chocolate melts**
**1 tblsp golden syrup**

1 Melt butter, chocolate and golden syrup together gently in a double boiler or microwave for 2 minutes. Stir to blend into a smooth paste. Set aside to cool but not set.
2 Once cold, whisk together into a fluffy thick frosting and lavish onto cakes.

## baby chocolate soufflé cakes

Delicately filled with air, these almost sponge-like baby cakes are soft and mellow.

**250g butter**
**250g chocolate**
**6 eggs, separated**
**1 cup sugar**
**1/2 cup plain flour**

1 Preheat oven to 160°C. Grease and flour 12 individual cake or muffin tins or one 20cm spring-form cake tin.
2 Melt butter and chocolate together in a double boiler, or microwave for 2 minutes.
3 Whisk egg yolks and sugar together briefly. Gently mix in melted butter and chocolate. Fold in sifted flour.
4 Whisk egg whites until soft peaks hold their shape. Fold egg whites into chocolate mixture.
5 Spoon into prepared tins and bake for 25 minutes or until a skewer inserted comes out clean.
6 Ice with chocolate ganache, page 17.

**Makes 12**

## complementary additions

- 1 cup fresh or frozen raspberries or blueberries folded into cake mix with egg whites.

## chocolate olive oil cakes

Cakes based on olive oil instead of butter tend to remain extraordinarily moist.

$^3/_4$ **cup fruity extra virgin olive oil**

**1 cup raw sugar**

**2 eggs**

$^1/_2$ **tsp salt**

**1 tsp vanilla extract**

$^1/_2$ **cup plain flour**

$^1/_2$ **cup self-raising flour**

**4 tblsp cocoa powder**

1  Preheat oven to 175°C. Grease and flour 10 individual cake or muffin tins or one 20cm spring-form cake tin.
2  Whisk oil, sugar, eggs, salt and vanilla together until creamy.
3  Sift together flours and cocoa, and fold into first mixture.
4  Spoon into prepared cake tins and bake for 20 minutes or until a skewer inserted comes out clean.
5  Cool a little before removing from tins. Drape with satin-like icing to serve.

**Makes 10**

## extra virgin chocolate icing

Rich and unctuous and definitely not for the faint-hearted.

**1 cup dark chocolate pieces**

$^1/_2$ **cup extra virgin olive oil**

1  Melt chocolate and olive oil together in a double boiler, or microwave for 2 minutes. Stir until smooth.

## flourless chocolate cakes

Ground almonds substitute for flour in this moist and decadent mixture.

**300g quality dark chocolate**
**250g butter**
**6 eggs, separated**
**1¼ cups sugar**
**2 tsp brandy**
**½ cup ground almonds**

1 Preheat oven to 170°C. Grease and flour 12 individual cake or muffin tins or one
   20cm spring-form cake tin.
2 Melt chocolate and butter together in a double boiler, or microwave for 2 minutes.
   Stir in 3/4 cup sugar and brandy and leave to cool to room temperature then stir
   in egg yolks.
3 Whisk egg whites until stiff peaks hold their shape. Beat in remaining 1/2 cup sugar.
   Fold meringue and ground almonds into chocolate mixture.
4 Divide between prepared tins and bake for 30 – 35 minutes or until a skewer inserted
   comes out clean.
5 Ice with chocolate ganache, page 17.

**Makes 12**

**syrup drenched**

### little madeira cakes with raspberry crush syrup

Raspberry crush sits prettily atop baby Madeira cakes either freely and casually draped or held in place by a formal paper collar.

125g butter

1 cup icing sugar

finely grated zest of 1 lemon

4 egg yolks

$^3/_4$ cup cornflour

1 tsp baking powder

$^1/_2$ cup milk

1 Preheat oven to 160°C. Grease and flour 12 individual cake or muffin tins or one 20cm spring-form cake tin.
2 Cream together butter, icing sugar, lemon zest and egg yolks. Stir in sifted dry ingredients and then milk.
3 Spoon into prepared tins and bake for 15 – 20 minutes or until a skewer inserted comes out clean.
4 Remove from tins to cool. Secure non-stick paper collars with string and saturate cakes with raspberry crush syrup.

Makes 12

### raspberry crush syrup

A berry solid crush cooked into a syrup that can also double as a sauce for ice-cream or a million other creations.

$1^1/_2$ cups sugar

$^1/_4$ cup water

juice of 3 lemons

300g raspberries (fresh or frozen)

1 Place sugar, water and lemon juice into a saucepan and bring to the boil, stirring until sugar has dissolved. Boil for 2 – 3 minutes.
2 Add raspberries and lightly crush. Boil for another 2 – 3 minutes. Pour over cakes.

## honey syrup gingerbread cakes

Ginger has always been a favourite flavour of mine since childhood so these little honeys are full of nostalgia.

| | |
|---|---|
| 60g butter | 1/2 tsp baking powder |
| 1/4 cup sugar | 2 tsp cinnamon |
| 1/2 cup treacle | 1 tblsp ground ginger |
| 1 1/2 cups boiling water | 1/2 tsp ground cloves |
| 3/4 tsp baking soda | 1/4 tsp salt |
| 1 1/2 cups plain flour | 1 large egg, beaten |

1   Preheat oven to 160°C. Grease and flour 10 individual cake or muffin tins or one 20cm spring-form cake tin.
2   Melt butter, sugar and treacle together. Add boiling water and baking soda and stir well.
3   Sift dry ingredients together then beat in first mixture until smooth. Lastly beat in egg.
4   Spoon into prepared tins and bake for 20 – 25 minutes or until a skewer inserted comes out clean. Remove to cool and serve drenched with honey syrup.

**Makes 10**

## honey syrup

A strong-flavoured honey will impart grand flavour to this syrup — try New Zealand manuka honey for example.

| | |
|---|---|
| 50g butter | 1/2 cup water |
| 1/2 cup liquid honey | 1 tsp vanilla extract |

1   Place all ingredients into a saucepan over a gentle heat until butter melts then boil for 1 minute. Sauce can be served hot or cold.

**Makes 1 cup**

## lemon sour cream cakes with lemon sugar

Soft baby lemon cakes sit happily under a crunchy sugar coating.

**125g butter**
**$^3/_4$ cup sugar**
**finely grated zest of one lemon**
**3 eggs**
**$^1/_2$ tsp lemon essence**
**$^1/_2$ cup sour cream**
**1 cup plain flour**
**1 tsp baking powder**

1  Preheat oven to 160°C. Grease and flour 12 individual cake or muffin tins or one 20cm spring-form cake tin.
2  Cream butter and sugar until pale. Beat in zest, eggs, lemon essence and sour cream. Fold in sifted dry ingredients. Pour into prepared tins and bake for 20 minutes or until a skewer inserted comes out clean.
3  Allow to cool before removing from cake tins. Spoon a little lemon sugar over each and this will soak in and set to form a crunchy crust.

**Makes 12**

## lemon sugar

This not-quite syrup remains sugar laden and forms a crunchy crystalline topping.

**juice of 3 lemons**
**$^1/_2$ cup caster sugar**

1  Mix juice and sugar together and drizzle over cakes as soon as they are removed from the oven.

## grape nectar baby cakes

Concentrating the sweet stickiness of grape juice forms honey-like nectar, which is simply stunning dribbled over little cakes.

$^3/_4$ cup caster sugar

finely grated zest of 2 lemons

125g butter

2 eggs

$^1/_2$ cup milk

$1^3/_4$ cups self-raising flour, sifted

$^1/_2$ cup raisins

1 Preheat oven to 160°C. Grease and flour 12 individual cake or muffin tins or one 20cm spring-form cake tin.

2 Cream sugar, zest and butter together. Beat in eggs and then milk. Gently stir in flour and raisins.

3 Divide between prepared tins and bake for 15–20 minutes or until a skewer inserted comes out clean. Cool.

4 Pour hot syrup over cold cakes to serve.

**Makes 12**

## grape nectar syrup

Perhaps this syrup of deep colour and flavour is nectar of the Gods!

$1^1/_2$ cups grape juice

juice of 1 lemon

1 cup sugar

1 Combine ingredients in a saucepan. Bring to the boil and then simmer for 10 minutes until thick and syrupy.

## whole orange cakes with orange syrup

Whole oranges are cooked down to a bitter pulp, which forms the basis of this citrus cake. Bizarre but true!

| | |
|---|---|
| 2 small oranges | $1/4$ cup semolina |
| 125g butter | $1/2$ cup ground almonds |
| $3/4$ cup caster sugar | 60g self-raising flour |
| 2 eggs | |

1 Preheat oven to 160°C. Grease and flour 12 individual cake or muffin tins or one 20cm spring-form cake tin.
2 Coarsely chop the oranges including the skin but remove any seeds. Place oranges in a saucepan with enough water to cover. Boil gently until oranges are tender and liquid has mostly reduced.
3 Blend or process cooled oranges until smooth.
4 Cream together butter and sugar until light and fluffy. Add eggs and beat well. Stir in the semolina, almonds, flour and then orange purée.
5 Divide mixture between prepared tins and bake for 30 minutes or until a skewer inserted comes out clean.
6 Pour hot orange syrup over cakes. Serve warm or cold.

**Makes 12**

## orange syrup

An almost intoxicating syrup full of the essence of oranges.

| | |
|---|---|
| 2 tblsp julienne orange zest | $1/2$ cup sugar |
| 1 cup orange juice | $1/4$ cup Cointreau |
| $1/4$ cup lemon juice | |

1 Place all ingredients into a saucepan. Bring to the boil then simmer until thick and syrupy.
2 Saturate cakes with orange syrup to serve.

## coconut rhubarb cakes with lemon syrup

Sweet coconut cakes easily hold the sharpness of rhubarb and lemon.

**125g butter**
**1 cup sugar**
**2 eggs**
**$^3/_4$ cup buttermilk (see page 17)**
**1$^1/_2$ cups self-raising flour**
**$^3/_4$ cup desiccated coconut**
**3 stalks rhubarb, roughly chopped**

1  Preheat oven to 160°C. Grease and flour 12 individual cake or muffin tins or one 20cm spring-form cake tin.
2  Cream butter and sugar, add eggs and beat well. Add buttermilk and beat to incorporate.
3  Stir in sifted flour, coconut and chopped rhubarb.
4  Spoon into prepared tins and bake for 20 – 25 minutes or until a skewer inserted comes out clean. Remove from tins to a rack to cool.
5  Once cold pour over hot lemon syrup.

**Makes 12**

## lemon syrup

A tart and juicy syrup that works well with many types of cake.

**juice of 6 lemons**
**$^1/_2$ cup water**
**1 cup sugar**

1  Combine ingredients in a saucepan. Bring to the boil, stirring until sugar dissolves. Boil for 1– 2 minutes until syrupy.

## chocolate opium baby cakes
Warning: poppy-seed laden cakes do tend to be addictive!

**125g butter, softened**
**1¼ cups sugar**
**4 eggs**
**125g chopped dark chocolate**
**¾ cup milk**
**1½ cups plain flour**
**½ cup cocoa powder**
**2½ tsp baking powder**
**½ cup poppy seeds**

1 Preheat oven to 160°C. Grease and flour 12 individual cake or muffin tins or one 20cm spring-form cake tin.
2 Cream butter and sugar until pale, beat in eggs. Melt chocolate in milk and whisk together until smooth. Stir in chocolate milk alternately with sifted dry ingredients and poppy seeds.
3 Pour into prepared tins and bake for 20 minutes or until a skewer inserted comes out clean.
4 Cool, remove from tins and drench in hot chocolate syrup.

**Makes 12**

## chocolate syrup
A liquid-satin syrup holding a touch of mocha.

**1½ cups coffee**
**100g chopped dark chocolate**
**¾ cup sugar**

1 Boil together in a pan until reduced to a light syrup. Pour hot syrup over cooled cakes.

## colombian coffee syrup cakes

Try these cakes served warm for dessert with an after-dinner coffee.

**250g butter**

**1¼ cups caster sugar**

**4 eggs**

**½ cup strong espresso coffee**

**2 tsp vanilla essence**

**1 tsp ground nutmeg**

**1 tblsp finely ground coffee beans**

**2¼ cups plain flour**

**1 tsp baking powder**

1  Preheat oven to 160°C. Grease and flour 12 individual cake or muffin tins or one 20cm spring-form cake tin.
2  Cream butter and sugar until pale and fluffy. Beat in eggs one at a time. Add espresso coffee, vanilla, nutmeg and ground coffee beans. Fold in sifted flour and baking powder.
3  Pour into prepared cake tins. Bake for 20 minutes or until a skewer inserted comes out clean. Cool in tins for 5 minutes before turning out onto a rack to cool completely. Pour hot syrup over cooled cakes.

**Makes 12**

## coffee syrup

Potent and direct, this syrup embraces its coffee cake counterparts perfectly.

**1½ cups strong coffee**

**¼ cup coffee liqueur**

**1 tsp ground coffee beans**

**¾ cup sugar**

1  Boil all ingredients together in a pan until reduced to a light syrup.

## passionfruit yoghurt syrup cakes

Refreshingly acidic and yet almost perfumed, passionfruit must be one of the best flavours in the world.

1 cup canola oil
1½ cups caster sugar
2 eggs
1 cup passionfruit yoghurt
juice and finely grated zest of 2 lemons
2 cups self-raising flour, sifted

1 Preheat oven to 160°C. Grease and flour 12 individual cake or muffin tins or one 20cm spring-form cake tin.

2 Whisk oil and sugar together to combine. Whisk in eggs until mixture is creamy, then stir in yoghurt, lemon juice and zest. Stir in flour until just mixed through. Try not to over-mix at this stage or the batter will become heavy and the resulting cakes will be hard and boring.

3 Spoon mixture into prepared tins and bake for 20 minutes or until a skewer inserted comes out clean.

4 Remove to a rack to cool and serve drenched in passionfruit syrup.

**Makes 12**

## passionfruit syrup

The pulp is the essence of the fruit, but strain out the seeds if you like.

½ cup lemon juice
½ cup water
1 cup sugar
½ cup passionfruit pulp

1 Place all ingredients into a saucepan and bring to the boil. Boil gently for 5 – 10 minutes until syrupy.

2 Pour hot syrup over cold cakes to serve.

**fruit and veg**

## carrot fruit salad cakes

The addition of fruit salad to a classic carrot cake causes it to become incredibly moist and exotic.

$^1/_2$ cup raw sugar

$^1/_2$ cup vegetable oil

1 tsp vanilla essence

2 eggs

$^1/_2$ cup canned fruit salad
  (preferably tropical-style),
  drained and chopped

1 ripe banana, mashed

1 cup grated carrot, firmly packed
  (about 1 large carrot)

$^3/_4$ cup self-raising flour

$^1/_4$ tsp salt

$^1/_2$ tsp baking soda

$^1/_4$ cup desiccated coconut threads

1 tblsp ground cinnamon

1 tsp allspice

1  Preheat oven to 175°C. Grease and flour 10 individual cake or muffin tins or one 20cm spring-form cake tin.

2  Whisk sugar, oil and vanilla together to combine. Add eggs one at a time beating until mixture is creamy. Stir in fruit salad, banana and grated carrot.

3  Add flour, salt, baking soda, coconut and spices. Stir to combine. Spoon cake mixture into prepared tins. Bake for 30 minutes or until a skewer inserted comes out clean.

4  Once cold, spread with lemon cream cheese icing.

**Makes 10**

## lemon cream cheese icing

The only appropriate topping for a carrot cake. Nothing else will do!

1 cup cream cheese, softened

50g butter, melted

$^1/_2$ cup caster sugar

finely grated zest of 1 lemon

1  Beat all ingredients together until creamy.

## little lemon meringue cakes

It has to be said that both Katie, our little hand model, and these wee cakes are the cutest of creations.

**1¹/₂ cups self-raising flour**          **4 tblsp milk**

**³/₄ cup caster sugar**          **juice and zest of 2 lemons**

**150g butter, softened**          **lemon curd (below)**

**3 eggs, lightly beaten**          **meringue (below)**

1  Preheat oven to 175°C. Prepare 12 paper cases.
2  Place first six ingredients into a bowl and beat until smooth and creamy. Spoon mixture to 3/4 fill cases. Bake for 20 minutes. Remove to a rack to cool. Reduce oven temperature to 120°C.
3  Once cold enough to handle, cut out a large cavity from the top of each cupcake and discard, or eat. Fill cavity with lemon curd. Spoon or pipe small mounds of meringue on top of lemon curd. Bake for 10 minutes further to set meringue.

### lemon curd

**75g butter**          **juice and zest of 2 lemons**

**¹/₂ cup sugar**          **2 eggs, beaten**

1  Place butter, sugar, lemon juice and zest into a double boiler. Stir over heat until sugar has dissolved. Whisk warm mixture into beaten eggs and return to double boiler. Cook over a low heat until mixture thickens to coat the back of a spoon.

### meringue

**2 egg whites**          **¹/₂ cup caster sugar**

1  Whisk egg whites until stiff. Add 1 tablespoonful of the sugar and whisk until incorporated. Whisk in remaining sugar until mixture is glossy.

**Makes 12**

## mango and lime cakes

Cakes with fruit make great dinner-party desserts. Dress this one up with a little mascarpone or cream, and serve some fresh berries or maybe passionfruit on the side.

**1 fresh mango sliced or 400g can mango pieces, drained**
**175g butter**
**³/₄ cup sugar**
**3 eggs**
**juice and finely grated zest of 2 limes**
**¹/₂ cup ground almonds**
**³/₄ cup plain flour**
**1 tsp baking powder**

1  Preheat oven to 160°C. Grease 12 individual cake or muffin tins or one 20cm spring-form cake tin. Arrange a few mango pieces on the bottom of each tin.

2  Cream together butter and sugar then beat in eggs. Stir in lime juice and zest. Fold in ground almonds, sifted flour and baking powder.

3  Spoon mixture over mangoes in prepared tins. Bake for 20 minutes or until a skewer inserted comes out clean.

4  Invert onto a rack while still hot so that mangoes don't stick to the bottom of the tins.

5  If you fancy, squeeze a little fresh lime juice over mangoes just before serving.

**Makes 12**

## chocolate zucchini mini cakes

Some people are slightly horrified at the inclusion of weird vegetables in sweet cakes but really they simply provide a bulk ingredient which adds moisture and texture to the cakes. Go on, give them a try!

3/4 **cup canola oil**

3/4 **cup sugar**

**2 eggs**

**250g zucchini (2 — 3 medium) trimmed,**
 **grated and squeezed to remove liquid**

1/2 **cup currants**

1/2 **cup wholemeal flour**

3/4 **cup plain flour**

**1 tsp baking powder**

1/2 **tsp baking soda**

1/4 **cup cocoa powder**

**2 tsp cinnamon**

**1 tsp nutmeg**

1/2 **tsp salt**

1  Preheat oven to 160°C. Grease and flour 12 individual cake or muffin tins or one 20cm spring-form cake tin.

2  Beat together oil, sugar and eggs until pale. Stir in grated zucchini, currants, wholemeal flour and remaining dry ingredients sifted together.

3  Spoon into prepared tins and bake for 20 — 25 minutes or until a skewer inserted comes out clean.

4  Cool in tins for 10 minutes before removing. Ice or dust with a mixture of cocoa powder and icing sugar to serve.

**Makes 12**

## pear olive oil spice cakes

Pungent spices combine beautifully with balmy sweet pears, and fruity olive oil lends these cakes an almost pudding-like texture.

| | |
|---|---|
| 1 cup olive oil | 1 tblsp cinnamon |
| 1 1/4 cups sugar | 1 tsp ground allspice |
| 2 eggs | 1 tsp ground ginger |
| 2 1/2 cups roughly cubed | 1 tsp baking soda |
| pears (cored but skin left on) | 1/2 cup chopped walnut pieces |
| 2 cups flour | |

1. Preheat oven to 160°C. Grease and flour 12 individual cake or muffin tins or one 20cm spring-form cake tin.
2. Whisk together oil, sugar and eggs until thick.
3. Place remaining ingredients into a large bowl, pour in wet ingredients and mix well to combine.
4. Divide between prepared tins and bake for 20 minutes or until a skewer inserted comes out a little moist but clean.
5. Drizzle with caramel glaze to serve.

**Makes 12**

## caramel glaze

Spooned over sweet baby cakes this glaze covers like a veil of caramel silk.

| | |
|---|---|
| 100g butter | 1 cup brown sugar, tightly packed |
| 1/2 cup cream | 1 tsp vanilla extract |

1. Place all ingredients into a saucepan and stir over a gentle heat until butter melts and sugar has dissolved.
2. Boil for 2 minutes until mixture is syrupy. Glaze can be served hot or cold.

**Makes 1 3/4 cups**

## banana and white chocolate chip cakes

Banana cakes would still have to be one of the most popular cakes for many folk. There are probably one hundred and one ways to vary this traditional cake; this is just one of them.

200g butter

1 cup sugar

3 eggs

3 mashed bananas

3 tblsp hot milk

1 tsp baking soda

1$\frac{3}{4}$ cups plain flour

1 tsp baking powder

1 tsp nutmeg

1 cup white chocolate bits

1 Preheat oven to 160°C. Grease and flour 12 individual cake or muffin tins or one 20cm spring-form cake tin.

2 Cream butter and sugar. Beat in eggs and bananas.

3 Stir in combined hot milk and baking soda. Gently stir in sifted dry ingredients and white chocolate bits.

4 Divide between prepared tins and bake for 20 minutes or until a skewer inserted comes out clean.

**Makes 12**

## topping ideas

- Ice with lemon icing, page 45.
- Top with chocolate frosting, page 18.
- Drizzle with caramel glaze, page 43.

## fresh plum and yoghurt baby cakes

Wonderfully damp and fruity, these cakes keep well but are best stored in the fridge because otherwise the fruit may tend to ferment. Sounds terrible and it would be a shame to sacrifice such cakes as these.

125g butter

1 cup sugar

3 eggs

finely grated zest of 1 lemon

1/2 cup plain yoghurt

2 cups plum slices (about 4 plums)

1 cup plain flour

1/2 cup self-raising flour

1 Preheat oven to 175°C. Grease and flour 16 individual cake or muffin tins or one 22cm spring-form cake tin.

2 Cream together butter and sugar until pale and fluffy. Beat in eggs and lemon zest. Stir in yoghurt and plum slices. Stir in flours sifted together.

3 Spoon into prepared tins and bake for 20 minutes or until a skewer inserted comes out clean.

4 Cool in tins a little before removing. Glaze with very thin lemon icing.

Makes 16

## lemon icing

A thin glassy icing that delicately clings to cakes and imparts a wonderful citrus tang.

1 cup icing sugar, sifted

juice of 1—3 lemons

1 Place icing sugar into a bowl and blend in just enough lemon juice to make a thin glassy icing.

## roast pumpkin spice cakes

Another damp, balmy sort of cake, these little gems also are suited to a dolloped topping of cream cheese icing.

1 small pumpkin, peeled and cubed

$^3/_4$ cup olive oil

1 cup sugar

2 eggs

1 tsp vanilla extract

1 tblsp ground cinnamon

$^1/_4$ tsp ground cloves

pinch salt

1 tsp baking powder

1 tsp baking soda

$^3/_4$ cup wholemeal flour

$^3/_4$ cup plain flour, sifted

$^1/_4$ cup pumpkin seeds, toasted

1 Preheat oven to 200°C. Place pumpkin cubes into an oven pan and dry roast for 20 minutes or until tender and caramelised. Cool and mash or purée. Measure 250g for cake.

2 Grease and flour 12 individual cake or muffin tins or one 20cm spring-form cake tin.

3 Beat oil and sugar together to blend then beat in eggs until thick and pale. Mix in pumpkin, vanilla, spices and salt. Stir in dry ingredients and pumpkin seeds.

4 Divide batter between prepared tins and bake for 30 minutes or until a skewer inserted comes out clean.

5 Turn out to cool then ice with lemon cream cheese icing, page 37.

**Makes 12**

# little sticky apricot pudding cakes

This ever-popular café favourite doubles as an irresistible pudding.

100g dried apricots, roughly chopped

100g pitted dates, roughly chopped

1 cup cold water

1 tsp baking soda

60g butter

2 tblsp golden syrup

$^1/_2$ cup brown sugar, tightly packed

1 tsp vanilla extract

2 eggs

$1^1/_2$ cups self-raising flour

1   Place apricots, dates and water into a saucepan and bring to the boil. Remove from heat and add baking soda. Set aside for fruit to soften and cool.

2   Preheat oven to 170°C. Grease and flour 12 individual cake or muffin tins or one 20cm spring-form cake tin.

3   Cream butter, golden syrup, sugar and vanilla together then beat in eggs.

4   Fold in sifted flour then stir in cooled fruit and liquid.

5   Pour into prepared tins and bake for 20 – 25 minutes or until skewer inserted comes out clean.

**Makes 12**

## serving suggestions

- Serve warm with caramel glaze, page 43.
- Serve hot with ice-cream.

nutty varieties

## sweet almond poppy seed cakes

The use of egg white instead of whole eggs makes a huge textural difference to these drop-dead gorgeous sweet little numbers.

125g butter, softened
3/4 cup caster sugar
grated zest of 1 orange
120g ground almonds
1/4 cup self-raising flour, sifted
1/4 cup poppy seeds
4 egg whites

1 Preheat oven to 170°C. Grease, flour and line with non-stick baking paper the base of 12 individual cake or muffin tins or one 20cm spring-form cake tin.
2 Cream together butter, sugar and orange zest until pale. Stir in ground almonds, flour and poppy seeds.
3 Whisk egg whites until soft peaks hold their shape. Fold 1/4 into the first mixture to lighten it then fold in the remaining egg whites until fully incorporated.
4 Spoon into prepared cake tins and bake for 15 minutes or until a skewer inserted comes out clean. Cool in tin for 5 minutes before turning out onto a rack. Ice once cold.

Makes 12

## poppy seed icing

More poppy seeds are a brilliant and logical topping for this cake.

1 cup icing sugar
1/4 cup poppy seeds
juice of 1 lemon

1 Blend all ingredients together until smooth, adding a little water if necessary to give a pouring consistency. Drizzle over cold cakes.

## nutmeg coconut baby cakes

Nutmeg is the most glorious aromatic and really makes these simple cakes quite unusual. I first made this recipe as a child in the farmhouse kitchen of a dear cousin.

125g butter

2 cups plain flour

2 tsp baking powder

pinch salt

1 cup brown sugar, tightly packed

1 tsp baking soda

1 cup milk

1 egg

2 tsp freshly grated nutmeg

1/2 cup desiccated coconut and a little extra for topping

1 Preheat oven to 180°C. Grease and flour 12 small cake or muffin tins or one 20cm spring-form cake tin.

2 Rub butter into flour then add baking powder, salt and brown sugar. Remove 4 heaped tablespoons of this mixture and divide this between the prepared tins. Press into bases of tins.

3 Dissolve baking soda in milk and add to remaining dry ingredients with the egg, nutmeg and coconut. Mix together to combine. Spoon evenly over prepared bases. Sprinkle with a little extra coconut. Bake for 15 minutes or until a skewer inserted comes out clean.

Makes 12

## almond, vanilla and raspberry friands

Friands are special French baby cakes that are always made with nuts and are probably the easiest cakes I know. They are also truly scrumptious to eat. What more could you want?

175g butter, melted

1 cup ground almonds

6 egg whites, lightly beaten

2 tsp vanilla extract

$1^1/_2$ cups icing sugar

$^1/_2$ cup plain flour

1 cup fresh raspberries (frozen are also fine)

1   Preheat oven to 190°C. Grease 10 individual cake or muffin tins.
2   Place all ingredients except raspberries into a mixing bowl. Stir until just combined.
3   Spoon mixture into prepared tins, they should be just over 1/2 full. Top each friand with 3 – 4 raspberries. Bake for 25 minutes.
3   Allow to stand in tins for 5 minutes before turning out onto a cooling rack.

Makes 10

### variations

- Friands always have ground nuts as a base ingredient but any variety of nuts can be used depending on your fancy.

# white chocolate and pecan spice friands

I think friands are great for morning or afternoon tea but also double beautifully as a stress-free pudding. Serve these hot with a scoop of ice-cream to melt over them.

100g butter

100g white chocolate melts

1 cup ground pecans (finely grind in a food processor)

6 egg whites, lightly beaten

$1^1/_2$ cups icing sugar

$^1/_2$ cup plain flour

1 tsp ground cinnamon

1 tsp ground allspice

1 Preheat oven to 190°C. Grease 10 individual cake or muffin tins.

2 Place butter and white chocolate together in a bowl and microwave on medium for 1–2 minutes or use a double boiler if you don't have a microwave.

3 Place all ingredients into a mixing bowl. Stir until just combined.

4 Spoon mixture into prepared tins; they should be just over 1/2 full. Bake for 25 minutes.

5 Allow to stand in tins for 5 minutes before turning out onto a cooling rack.

Makes 10

## variations

- Try these same friands using dark chocolate instead of white.
- Substitute coconut for the ground pecans to give coconut spice friands.

## hazelnut, chocolate and cherry friands

The wonderful flavours of chocolate and cherry seem to have a special affinity and work especially well in these hazelnut-based friands.

100g butter

100g quality dark chocolate

1 cup ground hazelnuts (finely grind in a food processor)

6 egg whites, lightly beaten

2 tsp vanilla extract

1$^1/_2$ cups icing sugar

$^1/_2$ cup plain flour

1 cup fresh pitted cherries (well-drained canned cherries are also fine)

1  Preheat oven to 190°C. Grease 10 individual cake or muffin tins.
2  Melt butter and chocolate together gently in a double boiler, or microwave for 1–2 minutes. Stir until smooth and place in a mixing bowl together with remaining ingredients. Stir until just combined.
3  Spoon mixture into prepared tins; they should be just over 1/2 full. Bake for 25 minutes.
4  Allow to stand in tins for 5 minutes before turning out onto a cooling rack.

Makes 10

### variations

- Any seasonal fruit can be used instead of cherries.
- Try any type of berry or stone fruit, as well as apples or pears or exotic fruits such as pineapple or mango.

## toasted coconut and banana friands

Obviously any kind of nut can be used in friands, even coconut. Coconut and bananas caramelise sweetly in the oven to release quite a different tropical flavour.

1/2 cup fine desiccated coconut

1/2 cup coconut threads, well packed

175g butter, melted

1 1/2 cups icing sugar

1/2 cup plain flour

6 egg whites

1/2 tsp coconut essence

1—2 bananas, sliced

1  Preheat oven to 190°C. Grease 10 individual cake or muffin tins.
2  Place both measures of coconut on an oven tray and toast in oven for 5 minutes, turning once, until golden. Cool.
3  Place all ingredients except bananas into a mixing bowl. Stir until just combined.
4  Spoon mixture into prepared tins to just over 1/2 full. Top each with a couple of banana slices. Bake for 25 minutes.
5  Allow to stand in tins for 5 minutes before turning out onto a cooling rack.

Makes 10

### variations

● Try topping these friands with different tropical fruit such as mango, papaya or pineapple slices.

## marzipan baby cakes

What an unexpected delight it is to find a sweet, moist, gooey centre of marzipan inside these plain cakes.

150g butter

1 cup caster sugar

3 eggs

1$^1$/$_2$ cups flour

3 tsp baking powder

$^3$/$_4$ cup ground almonds

$^3$/$_4$ cup milk

1 Preheat oven to 180°C. Grease and flour 15 individual cake or muffin tins or one 22cm spring-form cake tin.

2 Cream together butter and sugar, then beat in eggs until light and fluffy. Sift together flour and baking powder and combine with ground almonds. Add the dry ingredients alternately with the milk and stir to just combine.

3 Divide between prepared cake tins. Divide the marzipan into 15 equal portions and gently press one portion into each cake. Bake for 20 – 25 minutes or until a skewer inserted comes out clean. Remove to a rack to cool.

4 Pour over pink icing, see page 93, allowing it to just coat the cakes.

Makes 15

## marzipan

With such extraordinarily fragrant sweet almond stickiness, marzipan runs the risk of never making it into the cake mix.

$^1$/$_2$ cup ground almonds

$^1$/$_4$ cup pure icing sugar

1 tblsp egg white

1 – 2 drops almond or vanilla essence

1 Place almonds and icing sugar into a food processor. Process to combine, then with the motor running slowly add measured egg white and essence. Process until mixture comes together.

## roasted walnut cakes

Be sure to purchase the walnuts from a reliable source where the turnover of produce is high and you know they will be fresh. There is nothing worse than stale, manky walnuts.

125g fresh walnuts
125g butter, softened
1 cup caster sugar
3 eggs
1 cup self-raising flour
$^1/_2$ tsp baking powder
2 tblsp walnut oil

1  Preheat oven to 180°C. Spread walnuts onto a baking tray and roast for 5–10 minutes, shaking once, until golden brown. Remove to cool. Once walnuts are cold roughly chop until quite fine.
2  Grease and flour 12 individual cake or muffin tins or one 20cm spring-form cake tin.
3  Cream together butter and sugar and then beat in eggs one at a time. Stir in sifted flour and baking powder and lastly nuts and walnut oil.
4  Spoon into prepared cake tins and bake for 20 minutes or until a skewer inserted comes out clean.
5  Remove to a rack to cool. Serve drizzled with a little extra walnut oil if desired.

Makes 12

### variations

- You definitely have to like walnuts to be a fan of this cake, but then again hazelnuts, Brazil nuts or even pecans could be easily substituted.

# pistachio, date and chocolate meringue cakes

This mixture is incredibly stress-free to make and has very elaborate results in both taste and appearance.

3 egg whites

$^1/_4$ cup caster sugar

125g pistachio nuts, roughly chopped

125g dates, roughly chopped

125g quality dark chocolate, roughly chopped

1 Preheat oven to 160°C. Grease and dust with caster sugar 10 individual cake or muffin tins or one 20cm spring-form cake tin.

2 Whisk egg whites until soft peaks hold their shape. Add sugar and beat until incorporated. Fold in pistachios, dates and chocolate.

3 Spoon into prepared tins and bake for 30 minutes. Cool for 15 minutes in tins before removing.

4 Serve with fresh dates and pistachios or chocolate ganache, see page 17, if preferred.

Makes 10

## variations

- Use prunes, dried figs or apricots instead of the dates.
- Substitute almonds, walnuts or pecans for the pistachio nuts.
- Swap white chocolate or milk chocolate for the dark chocolate.

grains and rice

## chocolate risotto baby cakes

For this, the chocoholic's variety of rice cake, be sure to use the best quality chocolate and cocoa powder that you can afford.

2$^{1}/_{2}$ cups milk

2 tblsp sugar

2 tsp cocoa powder

50g butter

$^{3}/_{4}$ cup Italian risotto rice

2 eggs, separated

$^{1}/_{4}$ cup chopped toasted hazelnuts

$^{1}/_{4}$ cup chopped sultanas

75g grated quality dark chocolate

1 tblsp Frangelico or brandy

extra grated chocolate to decorate

1 Heat milk, sugar and cocoa together, stirring until sugar and cocoa dissolve.

2 Melt butter in a heavy-based pan, add risotto rice and stir over heat for 1 minute. Add hot milk mixture and stir to combine. Bring to the boil then cover and simmer for 20 minutes until milk has been mostly absorbed. Transfer to a bowl to cool.

3 Preheat oven to 160°C. Grease and flour 12 individual cake or muffin tins or one 20cm spring-form cake tin.

4 Mix egg yolks, hazelnuts, sultanas, chocolate and liqueur into cold rice. Whisk egg whites until soft peaks hold their shape and fold into chocolate risotto mixture.

5 Divide between prepared tins and bake for 15 minutes until golden and set. Cool before removing from tins.

6 Serve hot or chilled, decorated with extra grated chocolate.

**Makes 12**

## sticky wild rice cakes

Be certain to line the tins with non-stick baking paper because these rice cakes are terribly moist and hard to remove without a non-stick base.

$^1/_2$ **cup ground almonds**

$^1/_2$ **cup wild rice**

$^1/_4$ **tsp salt**

$^3/_4$ **cup water**

**400 ml can coconut milk**

$^1/_4$ **cup chopped crystallised ginger**

**2 eggs, lightly beaten**

$^1/_4$ **cup sugar**

$^1/_2$ **tsp vanilla extract**

1 Preheat oven to 160°C. Grease and line with non-stick baking paper the base of 10 individual cake or muffin tins or one 20cm spring-form cake tin and then sprinkle 1/4 cup of the ground almonds to coat the tins.

2 Place rice, salt and 3/4 cup water in a saucepan, bring to the boil and then simmer covered for 20 minutes until rice is just tender and all liquid has been absorbed. Add coconut milk and ginger and simmer uncovered for 10–15 minutes, stirring regularly until thick and most of the liquid has been absorbed. Remove mixture from heat; cool to room temperature.

3 Stir in eggs, sugar, vanilla and remaining 1/4 cup ground almonds.

4 Pour into prepared tins and bake for 25 minutes or until set. Cool before removing from tins.

**Makes 10**

## couscous cakes

The grainy texture of couscous is still evident in the finished product and this is fantastic because it really sets these couscous creations apart from any other cake type.

1/4 **cup rum or brandy**

1/2 **cup olive oil**

**finely grated zest and juice of 2 oranges**

**1 cup couscous**

**2 eggs**

3/4 **cup sugar**

1/2 **cup flour, sifted**

**2 tsp baking powder**

**2 tsp cinnamon**

1/4 **tsp salt**

3/4 **cup dried cranberries or sultanas**

1  Preheat oven to 170°C. Grease and flour 12 individual cake or muffin tins or one 20cm spring-form cake tin.

2  In a saucepan heat rum or brandy, oil, orange zest and juice. Place couscous in a bowl and pour over hot liquid. Cover with plastic wrap and leave to steam for 10 minutes. Uncover and fluff up couscous with a fork.

3  Whisk eggs and sugar together until thick and pale. Stir this mixture into couscous along with remaining dry ingredients and cranberries or sultanas.

4  Spoon into prepared tins and bake for 15 minutes or until cakes spring back when touched.

**Makes 12**

## crunchy polenta fruit cakes

Fruit cakes are one of the best types of cake, well in my opinion anyway. The consistency of this one is pleasingly soft and moist in juxtaposition to the crunch of the polenta.

150g butter

$^3/_4$ cup caster sugar

3 eggs, beaten

$^3/_4$ cup self-raising flour, sifted

$1^1/_2$ tsp baking powder

$^1/_2$ cup instant (pre-cooked) polenta (cornmeal)

$^1/_2$ cup raisins

$^1/_2$ cup currants

$^1/_2$ cup chopped dried apricots

4 tblsp milk

juice and finely grated zest of 1 lemon

1 Preheat oven to 160°C. Grease and flour 12 individual cake or muffin tins or one 20cm spring-form cake tin.
2 Cream together butter and sugar until pale and fluffy. Beat in eggs to combine.
3 Fold in flour, baking powder and polenta. Stir in dried fruits, milk, lemon juice and zest.
4 Spoon into prepared tins and bake for 20 minutes or until a skewer inserted comes out clean. Remove and cool in tins before turning out.

Makes 12

## semolina ricotta cakes

Perceptibly citrus scented and a little sandy in texture, this Austrian-style curd cake is perfect served faintly warm.

**150g butter**
**1¹/₂ cups sugar**
**4 eggs, separated**
**600g ricotta**
**1 tsp vanilla extract**
**finely grated zest and juice of 2 lemons**
**³/₄ cup semolina**
**¹/₂ cup ground almonds and extra for dusting**
**¹/₂ cup dried currants**

1  Preheat oven to 160°C. Grease 12 individual cake or muffin tins or one 20 cm spring-form cake tin and dust with extra ground almonds.
2  Cream butter and sugar until pale. Beat in egg yolks, ricotta, vanilla, zest and juice. Fold in semolina, ground almonds and currants and mix well.
3  Whisk egg whites to soft peaks and gently fold into cake mixture.
4  Pour into prepared cake tins. Bake for 20 minutes or until a skewer inserted comes out clean.

**Makes 12**

## sticky bran fruit cakes

The sticky texture of these incredibly good, almost healthy cakes will make up for any reservations there may be about the use of bran in this recipe.

1 cup flour

2 tsp baking powder

$^{1}/_{2}$ cup brown sugar, tightly packed

$^{1}/_{2}$ tsp salt

$^{1}/_{2}$ tsp baking soda

1 tsp cinnamon

$^{1}/_{2}$ tsp cloves

$^{1}/_{4}$ cup chopped dried apricots

1 cup bran flakes

50g butter

3 tblsp golden syrup

1 ripe banana, mashed

$^{3}/_{4}$ cup milk

1 egg, beaten

1 Preheat oven to 190°C. Grease and flour 12 individual cake or muffin tins or one 20cm spring-form cake tin.

2 Place all the dry ingredients together in a bowl and make a well in the centre of these ingredients.

3 Melt butter and golden syrup together, mix with remaining wet ingredients and pour into the well. Stir briefly to just combine.

4 Spoon into prepared tins and bake for 15–20 minutes or until a skewer inserted comes out clean.

**Makes 12**

## oat and apple streusel cakes

Crunchy streusel topping sits well atop these wonderfully damp and balmy oat-based apple cakes.

60g butter
1/2 tsp baking soda
2 tsp cinnamon
1/2 cup brown sugar,
  tightly packed
1 apple, grated (you can
  leave the skin on)

1/2 cup raisins
1/2 cup milk
1 egg, beaten
1/2 cup rolled oats
3/4 cup plain flour
1 1/2 tsp baking powder

1  Preheat oven to 175°C. Grease and flour 10 individual cake or muffin tins or one 20cm spring-form cake tin.
2  Place butter, baking soda, cinnamon, sugar, apples, raisins and milk into a saucepan and bring to the boil, stirring until sugar dissolves and butter melts. Remove to cool.
3  Beat in egg. Add oats, sifted flour and baking powder and stir to combine. Spoon mixture into prepared pans, sprinkle with streusel topping and bake for 20 minutes or until springy to the touch. Cool in tins for 10 minutes before turning out.
4  Dust with icing sugar to serve.

**Makes 10**

## streusel topping

50g butter, cubed
1/2 cup plain flour
1/4 cup sugar
1/2 tsp ground cinnamon

1  Rub butter into flour until crumbly. Stir in sugar and cinnamon. Sprinkle over cakes before baking.

## little citrus rice cakes

These are my version of the traditional Italian Torta di Riso, and are rather like a rice pudding set in cake form. Berries complement them particularly beautifully.

2 tblsp olive oil

1 cup Italian risotto rice

3½ cups warmed milk

¼ cup ground almonds (to dust cake tins)

2 eggs

½ cup sugar

grated zest and juice of one lemon

1 Heat oil in a heavy-based pan, add risotto rice and stir for one minute to lightly toast. Add milk and bring to the boil then simmer over a moderate heat, stirring regularly to prevent sticking, until the rice is tender and the milk is absorbed (about 20 minutes). Transfer to a bowl to cool.

2 Preheat oven to 160°C. Grease 12 individual cake or muffin tins or one 20cm spring-form cake tin and sprinkle with ground almonds.

3 Whisk eggs and sugar until very thick and pale. Fold egg mixture, zest and juice into cold rice mixture.

4 Divide mixture between prepared tins and bake for 15 minutes or until golden and set. Cool before carefully removing from tins.

**Makes 12**

## polenta pinenut cakes

Not at all fancy but with good strong Italian flavours, this cake is always popular.

1$^1/_4$ cups thick yoghurt
$^1/_2$ cup polenta
juice and grated zest of 1 orange
125g butter, softened
1 cup caster sugar
3 eggs
1$^1/_4$ cups self-raising flour
$^1/_2$ tsp baking soda
$^1/_4$ cup pinenuts
$^1/_4$ cup currants
finely grated zest and juice of 2 oranges
3 tblsp sugar

1 Combine yoghurt, polenta, orange juice and zest and leave to stand for 2 hours for polenta to soften.
2 Preheat oven to 160°C. Grease and flour 12 individual cake or muffin tins or one 20cm spring-form cake tin.
3 Cream butter and sugar then beat in eggs. Fold in sifted flour and baking soda. Gently fold in yoghurt mixture, pinenuts and currants. Spoon into prepared cake tins and bake for 25 minutes or until a skewer inserted comes out clean.
4 While still hot, immediately drizzle with orange zest and juice mixed with sugar.

**Makes 12**

bread and butter

## croissant, blueberry and almond baby cakes

In the case of croissants the addition of butter is not necessary because croissants are already lusciously brimming with butter.

**8 stale croissants**

**1 cup blueberries, fresh or frozen**

**$^1/_2$ cup ground almonds**

**3 eggs**

**pinch salt**

**1 cup milk**

**$^1/_2$ cup cream**

**few drops almond essence or vanilla extract**

**1 cup sugar**

**$^1/_4$ cup flaked almonds**

1  Preheat oven to 160°C. Grease 12 individual cake or muffin tins or one 20cm spring-form cake tin.

2  Slice and layer or pack croissants into prepared tins interspersing with blueberries and ground almonds. Press down well.

3  Beat eggs, salt, milk, cream, vanilla and sugar together. Pour evenly over cakes, leave to rest for 1/2 hour for bread to completely absorb liquid. Sprinkle with flaked almonds.

4  Bake for 30 minutes. Cakes will inflate slightly when cooked, deflating again once cold. Cool a little before removing from tins. Serve warm or cold.

**Makes 12**

## mini coconut and apricot bread and butter cakes

Made by this method, the intrinsically pudding-like mixture of bread and butter, flavourings and soft custard is controlled and shaped into little cakes.

1 cup chopped dried apricots

$^1/_4$ cup sherry

10 – 12 slices stale white sandwich bread

50g butter, softened

$^1/_2$ cup desiccated coconut threads

3 eggs

pinch salt

400ml can coconut cream

few drops coconut essence

$^3/_4$ cup sugar

1 Preheat oven to 160°C. Grease 12 individual cake or muffin tins or one 20cm spring-form cake tin. Soak apricots in sherry for 1–2 hours.

2 Butter bread (I like to leave the crusts on) and layer in prepared tins alternating with a sprinkling of coconut and sherry soaked apricots. Press down well. Make sure top layer of bread is attractively arranged.

3 Beat eggs, salt, coconut cream, essence and sugar together. Pour evenly over cakes and leave to rest for 1/2 hour for bread to completely absorb liquid.

4 Bake for 30 minutes. Cakes will inflate slightly when cooked, deflating again once cold. Cool a little before removing from tins. Serve warm or cold.

Makes 12

## panettone and prune baby cakes

Using stale bread is best in these cakes because it will readily soak up the added liquid. Panettone is an Italian celebration bread, and it gives fantastic flavour and fabric to this style of cake, but of course, any other bread can be substituted.

10 – 12 thin slices stale panettone

50g butter, softened

1 cup pitted prunes, roughly chopped

3 eggs

pinch salt

$1^1/_2$ cups milk

$^3/_4$ cup sugar

1  Preheat oven to 160°C. Grease 12 individual cake or muffin tins or one 20cm spring-form cake tin.
2  Butter bread and layer in prepared tins alternating with a sprinkling of prunes. Press down well. Make sure top layer of bread is attractively arranged.
3  Beat eggs, salt, milk, and sugar together. Pour evenly over cakes and leave to rest for 1/2 hour for bread to completely absorb liquid.
4  Bake for 30 minutes. Cakes will inflate slightly when cooked, deflating again once cold. Cool a little before removing from tins. Serve warm or cold.

Makes 12

## white chocolate and quince sourdough bread and butter cakes

Quince paste is a wonderfully useful ingredient and adds a concentrated fruity flavour to these cakes. Quince and other fruit pastes are easy to make but are also readily obtainable from specialist food stores.

10—12 thin slices stale sourdough from a large loaf

50g butter, softened

1 cup white chocolate, roughly chopped (or use chocolate melts)

1/2 cup quince paste, roughly chopped

3 eggs

pinch salt

1 1/2 cups milk

3/4 cup sugar

1  Preheat oven to 160°C. Grease 12 individual cake or muffin tins or one 20cm spring-form cake tin.

2  Butter bread (remove the crusts if you prefer) and layer in prepared tins alternating with a sprinkling of white chocolate and chopped quince paste. Press down well. Make sure top layer of bread is attractively arranged.

3  Beat eggs, salt, milk, and sugar together. Pour evenly over cakes, leave to rest for 1/2 hour for bread to completely absorb liquid.

4  Bake for 30 minutes. Cakes will inflate slightly when cooked, deflating again once cold. Cool a little before removing from tins. Serve warm or cold.

Makes 12

### substitution

- Sourdough gives a strong texture and slightly sour flavour to these cakes but any other type of bread would make a good substitute.

## rum and raisin brown bread and butter baby cakes

Of course, these cakes can still be served as a pudding. To be at their best they should still hold a memory of warmth or at least be vaguely reheated and then served with maybe a little cream or ice-cream.

10—12 stale slices grainy brown bread
50g butter, softened
1 cup raisins
3 eggs
pinch salt
1 cup milk
$1/4$ cup cream
$1/4$ cup rum
$3/4$ cup brown sugar, tightly packed

1 Preheat oven to 160°C. Grease 12 individual cake or muffin tins or one 20cm spring-form cake tin.

2 Butter bread (I like to leave the crusts on) and layer in prepared tins alternating with a sprinkling of raisins. Press down well. Make sure top layer of bread is attractively arranged.

3 Beat eggs, salt, milk, cream, rum and sugar together. Pour evenly over cakes, leave to rest for 1/2 hour for bread to completely absorb liquid.

4 Bake for 30 minutes. Cakes will inflate slightly when cooked, deflating again once cold. Cool a little before removing from tins. Serve warm or cold.

Makes 12

## banana and maple fruit bread and butter cakes

Bread and butter cakes are really very accommodating. Vary the flavours as you wish. Any additions can be made according to your liking or whatever you have at hand that would combine into the mixture.

12—14 stale slices fruit bread, crusts removed

50g butter, softened

2 bananas, sliced

3 eggs

pinch salt

1 cup milk

1/4 cup cream

1/2 cup maple syrup

1/4 cup raw sugar

1   Preheat oven to 160°C. Grease 12 individual cake or muffin tins or one 20cm spring-form cake tin.

2   Butter bread and layer in prepared tins interspersing with sliced banana. Press down well. Make sure top layer of bread is attractively arranged.

3   Beat eggs, salt, milk, cream and maple syrup together. Pour evenly over cakes, leave to rest for 1/2 hour for bread to completely absorb liquid.

4   Sprinkle with raw sugar.

5   Bake for 30 minutes. Cakes will inflate slightly when cooked, deflating again once cold. Cool a little before removing from tins. Serve warm or cold.

Makes 12

# french toast, cinnamon and apple petit cakes

French toast for breakfast, and now as a cake combination; blurred memories of flavours and childhood combine into what has now become a café classic.

3 tblsp ground cinnamon

100g butter, softened

1 stale French stick, sliced

2 apples, grated

3 eggs

pinch salt

1 cup milk

1/2 cup cream

1 tsp vanilla extract

3/4 cup sugar

1 Preheat oven to 160°C. Grease 12 individual cake or muffin tins or one 20cm spring-form cake tin.
2 Mix cinnamon and butter together and spread over slices of French bread. Layer bread in prepared tins alternating with a little grated apple. Press down well. Make sure top layer of bread is attractively arranged.
3 Beat eggs, salt, milk, cream, vanilla and sugar together. Pour evenly over cakes and leave to rest for 1/2 hour for bread to completely absorb liquid.
4 Bake for 30 minutes. Cakes will inflate slightly when cooked, deflating again once cold. Cool a little before removing from tins. Serve warm or cold.

Makes 12

## madeira, vanilla and peach baby cakes

To be clever here is a bread and butter cake made with cake instead of bread. The cake can be stale, and in fact is probably better to be so. It will soak up the custard more easily this way.

1 small Madeira cake, thinly sliced
1 cup peach slices (fresh or canned are fine)
50g butter, melted
3 eggs
pinch salt
1 cup milk
$^1/_4$ cup cream
$^3/_4$ cup sugar
zest and juice of 2 oranges

1  Preheat oven to 160°C. Grease 12 individual cake or muffin tins or one 20cm spring-form cake tin.
2  Layer sliced Madeira in prepared tins with peach slices. Press down well. Drizzle with melted butter.
3  Beat eggs, salt, milk, cream, sugar, orange zest and juice together. Pour evenly over cakes and leave to rest for 1/2 hour for cakes to completely absorb liquid.
4  Bake for 30 minutes. Cakes will inflate slightly when cooked, deflating again once cold. Cool a little before removing from tins. Serve warm or cold.

Makes 12

● Use bought Madeira or make the superior recipe on page 25!

## little brioche, pear and chocolate cakes

Any kind of bread can be used in any version of bread and butter pudding cakes but I find brioche works incredibly well because it already has a buttery sweetness.

12 slices stale brioche

4 pears, cored and sliced

1 cup quality dark chocolate, roughly chopped

50g butter, melted

3 eggs

pinch salt

1 cup milk

1/4 cup cream

1/4 cup pear liqueur or brandy

1/2 cup brown sugar, tightly packed

1 Preheat oven to 160°C. Grease 12 individual cake or muffin tins or one 20cm spring-form cake tin.

2 Layer or pack brioche in prepared tins interspersing with pear slices and chocolate. Drizzle with melted butter.

3 Beat eggs, salt, milk, cream, liqueur and sugar together. Pour evenly over cakes, leave to rest for 1/2 hour for brioche to completely absorb liquid.

4 Bake for 30 minutes. Cakes will inflate slightly when cooked, deflating again once cold. Cool a little before removing from tins. Serve warm or cold.

Makes 12

# cheesecakes

## classic new york cheesecakes

Pure good cheesecake is classic. However, there is often hot debate as to whether the base should be of biscuit crumbs or pastry, but either tastes good and works well really — it's all down to personal preference.

**250g packet plain sweet biscuits**

**$1/4$ cup sugar**

**125g butter, melted**

**500g cream cheese at room temperature**

**$3/4$ cup sugar**

**$3/4$ cup sour cream**

**2 large eggs**

**juice and finely grated zest of 1 orange**

1 Preheat oven to 160°C. Line with baking paper and grease 12 individual cake or muffin tins or one 20cm spring-form cake tin.

2 Place biscuits and first measure of sugar into the bowl of a food processor and pulse to form crumbs. Add butter and process to combine. Press crumbs into the base and sides of prepared tins. Chill well while preparing filling.

3 Beat cream cheese and second measure of sugar together until smooth. Add remaining ingredients and beat well to combine. Pour into prepared crusts. Bake for 30 minutes or until set. Cool in oven with door ajar. Refrigerate for several hours to firm before serving.

**Makes 12**

## variations

- Add 1/2 cup chopped afterdinner mints for a choc mint cheesecake (remove orange for this variation).
- Add 1/2 cup chocolate chips for a jaffa cheesecake.

## little polka dot cheesecakes

The polka dot concept is Maida Heatter's; the recipe is an adaptation of hers. She says that nothing gives her such pleasure as this cake — it is a true sensual delight.

**200g sweet shortcrust pastry**
**100g chopped quality dark chocolate**
**500g cream cheese at room temperature**
**1 cup caster sugar**
**1 tsp vanilla extract**
**2 large eggs**

1  Preheat oven to 150°C. Grease 12 individual cake rings or one 20cm spring-form cake tin.
2  Roll out pastry to 4mm thick and use to line the base of tins. Prick pastry and chill well. Melt chocolate over a gentle heat and set aside to cool a little.
3  Cream together cream cheese and sugar until smooth and fluffy. Add vanilla and eggs and beat to combine. Reserve 1/4 of the mixture; add melted chocolate to this and beat to combine then place into a piping bag fitted with a large plain nozzle.
4  Pour the bulk of the cheesecake mixture into the prepared tins. Insert piped dots of chocolate deeply and evenly into each cake. These will look like polka dots when the cakes are cut.
5  Bake for 25 minutes or until set but not dry.
6  Cool in tins before carefully removing.

**Makes 12**

## cream cheese and hidden berry cup cakes

Another kind of cake containing cheese but in an unexpected fashion.

**100g butter**
**¹/₂ cup sugar**
**4 eggs**
**¹/₂ cup plain flour**
**¹/₂ cup custard powder**
**1 tsp baking powder**
**¹/₂ cup cream cheese**
**fresh raspberries**

1 Preheat oven to 175°C. Grease and flour 10 individual cake or muffin tins.
2 Cream butter and sugar until pale then beat in eggs. Stir in sifted dry ingredients.
3 Spoon part of the mixture into prepared tins so that they are 1/2 full. Top with a teaspoonful of cream cheese and a couple of raspberries. Cover with remaining cake mixture.
4 Bake for 20 minutes or until springy to the touch.
5 Ice with pink icing.

**Makes 10**

## pink icing

As pretty as a picture but only if you opt for a delicate shade of pink.

**1 cup icing sugar**          **1 drop red food colouring**
**1 tblsp lemon juice**

1 Mix all ingredients with just enough hot water to form a smooth, flowing icing.

## petit pashka

Pashka is a traditional Russian Easter dessert with a creamy cheesy texture and contains dried fruit, nuts and chocolate. Don't be put off by the muslin wrapping/hanging procedure because this divine mixture is ridiculously easy to make.

**1 cup cream cheese at room temperature**
**1 cup quark**
**50g butter, softened**
**2 egg yolks**
**$1/2$ cup caster or vanilla sugar**
**$1/4$ cup chopped dried apricots**
**$1/4$ cup chopped quality dark chocolate**
**$1/4$ cup chopped almonds or pistachio nuts**
**grated zest and juice of one lemon**
**1 tsp vanilla extract**
**1 metre muslin, cut into eight**

1 Beat cream cheese, quark, butter, yolks and sugar together until smooth. Stir in remaining ingredients.
2 Sterilise 8 small pieces or one large piece of muslin by boiling in water for 2 minutes. Remove, cool and wring out muslin. Lay wet muslin inside 8 tea cups and place mixture in centre. Bring together ends of cloth and tie with string. Hang muslin bundles from string in fridge for 24 hours or more to drain and set. Place a container under pashka to catch moisture.
3 Unwrap pashka and serve with fresh fruit.

**Makes 8**

## vanilla sugar

- Vanilla sugar is simply made by placing 1 — 2 whole vanilla pods in caster sugar. Stored in an airtight container the sugar will absorb the deliciously strong flavour of vanilla.

## strawberry cheesecakes

Real strawberries contain a heady perfect flavour and all the warmth of the summer sun. Thankfully, strawberries are once again tasting as they should.

200g sweet shortcrust pastry

300g strawberries, hulled

3 tblsp Kirsch or brandy

$^3/_4$ cup caster sugar

500g cream cheese
 at room temperature

$^1/_2$ cup sour cream

2 eggs, separated

2 tblsp powdered gelatine

5 tblsp hot water

fresh strawberries to decorate

1  Preheat oven to 190°C. Line with baking paper and grease 12 individual cake or muffin tins or one 22cm spring-form cake tin.

2  Roll out pastry and use to line the base of prepared tins. Prick pastry and chill well then bake for 5 – 8 minutes until golden brown. Form paper collars inside the tins so that cheesecakes will be easy to remove.

3  Purée strawberries with Kirsch and sugar in a food processor. Add cream cheese, sour cream and egg yolks and process well to combine into a smooth mixture.

4  Sprinkle gelatine over measured hot water in a small bowl or cup and leave to swell. Heat bowl of prepared gelatine in a water bath, or microwave oven for 40 seconds to dissolve. Stir into strawberry mixture.

5  Whisk egg whites until stiff peaks form and gently fold into filling. Pour into prepared tins and refrigerate overnight to set. Turn out and decorate with fresh strawberries to serve.

**Makes 12**

## flavouring alternatives

● Any berry can be substituted for the strawberries or use a mixture of berries. Apricot, peach or plum purée works well.

## lemon curd ricotta cheesecakes

Ricotta still retains a delicate curd texture that mingles with the lemon curd and yields light, low-fat cakes perfect to sit exotic fruits upon.

**75g butter**
**1/2 cup sugar**
**finely grated zest and juice of 2 lemons**
**2 eggs, beaten**
**300g ricotta**
**trifle sponge (available from supermarkets)**
**fresh seasonal fruit to decorate**

1  Place butter, sugar, lemon juice and zest into a double boiler. Stir over heat until sugar has dissolved and mixture is warm. Whisk warm mixture into beaten eggs and return to double boiler. Cook over a low heat until mixture thickens to coat the back of a spoon. Do not allow the mixture to boil or it will curdle. Set aside to cool.
2  Beat cold lemon mixture with ricotta until smooth.
3  Thinly slice sponge and cut out eight 6cm circle bases. Wrap strips of waxed paper around sponge bases and paperclip or staple to secure. Pack each case firmly with lemon ricotta mixture. Chill well to set.
4  Decorate with fresh seasonal fruit to serve.

**Serves 8**

### delicious fruit to decorate

- A bunch of cherries with their stems.
- A few red or green grapes.
- Sliced mango, melon, pineapple or pawpaw.
- Any fresh and fragrant berries dusted with icing sugar.
- Sliced stone fruits drizzled with liqueur.

## little apricot cheesecakes with white chocolate

Chunks of ingredients like dried apricots can sometimes cause cakes to turn out pleasurably irregular, and this is a good thing.

**400g sweet shortcrust pastry**

**1/2 cup white chocolate melts**

**1/4 cup cream**

**1/2 cup cream cheese**

**1 tblsp sugar**

**1 egg**

**1/2 cup chopped dried apricots**

**1 1/2 cups white chocolate melts to cover**

1 Roll out pastry to 3mm thick, use a pastry cutter to cut out rounds and use to line 12 muffin tins or 24 tiny tins. Prick bases and chill well.

2 Preheat oven to 190°C. Line pastry shells with baking paper or foil and fill with baking beans. Bake pastry for 10 minutes. Remove beans and cool pastry. Reduce oven temperature to 150°C.

3 Melt first measure of white chocolate and cream together carefully for 1 1/2 minutes in microwave or in a bowl over boiling water. Beat cream cheese and sugar together until smooth, beat in egg. Mix in melted chocolate and apricots. Spoon into pastry shells. Bake for 15 minutes or until just set.

4 To some this may seem totally unnecessary but the top of each baby cheesecake can be lightly covered with melted white chocolate if you fancy. To do this, carefully melt second measure of white chocolate and spread a thin coating over each cake.

**Makes 12 small cakes or 24 teeny tiny cakes**

## espresso cheesecakes

Adding freshly ground coffee beans may seem unusual but they add a true flavour of coffee and a pleasant textural dimension. Good quality coffee is a requisite in this intense construction.

**200g digestive biscuits**
**$^1/_4$ cup sugar**
**1 tsp cinnamon**
**100g butter, melted**

**filling:**
**1 tblsp powdered gelatine**
**$^1/_2$ cup boiling water**
**300g cream cheese**
**$^1/_2$ cup sugar**
**200g dark chocolate**
**1 cup hot strong espresso coffee**
**$1^1/_4$ cups cream, whipped**

1  Crush biscuits in a food processor or with a rolling pin. Mix with sugar, cinnamon and melted butter. Spread evenly into the base of twelve 6cm-cake rings or a 20cm spring-form cake tin and press down well. Wrap a paper collar around the inside of the tins to enclose the filling.

2  Sprinkle gelatine over measured boiling water in a small bowl or cup and leave to swell.

3  Beat cream cheese and sugar together until smooth. Melt chocolate in hot coffee, stir until smooth and beat into cream cheese mixture.

4  Heat bowl of prepared gelatine in a water bath, or microwave oven for 40 seconds to dissolve. Mix well into filling.

5  Allow mixture to cool before folding in whipped cream. Pour over prepared bases and refrigerate for at least 6 hours to set.

**Makes 12**

## bambini tiramisu

Literally translated to mean 'pick-me-up', these little babies will certainly do the trick.

**200g trifle sponge (available from supermarkets)**

**3 egg yolks**

**¼ cup sugar**

**1 vanilla pod**

**300g mascarpone**

**¼ cup strong espresso coffee**

**¼ cup coffee-flavoured liqueur**

**10 crushed Amaretti biscuits**

**100g dark chocolate, grated**

1 Line 10 individual cake tins or cups with plastic wrap for ease of removal. Slice sponge into thin layers and cut out circles to fit cake moulds (a pastry cutter works well).

2 Split the vanilla pod and remove the seeds. Beat egg yolks, sugar and vanilla seeds together in a bowl over simmering water until thick and pale. Remove from heat and beat until cool. Beat in mascarpone.

3 Layer sponge drizzled with coffee and liqueur into moulds alternately with mascarpone mix. Chill well.

4 Remove carefully and serve topped with a sprinkling of crushed Amaretti biscuits and grated chocolate.

**Makes 10**

**index**

### straight chocolate

chocolate lamington baby cakes 12

baby chocolate soufflé cakes 19

chocolate olive oil cakes 20

flourless chocolate cakes 22

little chocolate bleeding hearts 15

little chocolate brownie cakes 16

mini chocolate fudge cakes 18

sour cream cocoa cakes 11

spiced chocolate buttermilk cakes 17

### syrup drenched

chocolate opium baby cakes 32

coconut rhubarb cakes with lemon syrup 31

colombian coffee syrup cakes 33

grape nectar baby cakes 28

honey syrup gingerbread cakes 26

lemon sour cream cakes with lemon sugar 27

little madeira cakes with raspberry
 crush syrup 25

passionfruit yoghurt syrup cakes 34

whole orange cakes with orange syrup 30

### fruit and veg

banana and white chocolate chip cakes 44

carrot fruit salad cakes 37

chocolate zucchini mini cakes 42

fresh plum and yoghurt baby cakes 45

little lemon meringue cakes 38

little sticky apricot pudding cakes 48

mango and lime cakes 41

pear olive oil spice cakes 43

roast pumpkin spice cakes 46

### nutty varieties

almond, vanilla and raspberry friands 53

hazelnut, chocolate and cherry friands 55

marzipan baby cakes 58

nutmeg coconut baby cakes 52

pistachio, date and chocolate meringue
 cakes 60

roasted walnut cakes 59

sweet almond poppy seed cakes 51

toasted coconut and banana friands 56

white chocolate and pecan spice friands 54

### grains and rice

chocolate risotto baby cakes 63

couscous cakes 67

crunchy polenta fruit cakes 68

little citrus rice cakes 72

oat and apple streusel cakes 71

polenta pinenut cakes 74

semolina ricotta cakes 69

sticky bran fruit cakes **70**
sticky wild rice cakes **64**

**bread and butter**
banana and maple fruit bread
 and butter cakes **83**
croissant, blueberry and almond
 baby cakes **77**
french toast, cinnamon and apple
 petit cakes **84**
little brioche, pear and chocolate cakes **86**
madeira, vanilla and peach baby cakes **85**
mini coconut and apricot bread
 and butter cakes **78**
panettone and prune baby cakes **79**
rum and raisin brown bread
 and butter baby cakes **82**
white chocolate and quince sourdough
 bread and butter cakes **80**

**cheesecakes**
bambini tiramisu **101**
classic new york cheesecakes **89**
cream cheese and hidden berry cup cakes **93**
espresso cheesecakes **100**
lemon curd ricotta cheesecakes **97**
little apricot cheesecakes with
 white chocolate **98**
little polka dot cheesecakes **90**
petit pashka **94**
strawberry cheesecakes **95**

**icings, syrups and toppings**
caramel glaze **43**
chocolate coconut coating **12**
chocolate frosting **18**
chocolate ganache **17**
chocolate syrup **32**
coffee syrup **33**
extra virgin chocolate icing **20**
grape nectar syrup **28**
honey syrup **26**
lemon cream cheese icing **37**
lemon curd **38**
lemon icing **45**
lemon sugar **27**
lemon syrup **31**
marzipan **58**
meringue **38**
orange syrup **30**
passionfruit syrup **34**
pink icing **93**
poppy seed icing **51**
raspberry crush syrup **25**
streusel topping **71**